Paddle Through the Watery Depths of

SEALS &
SEA LIONS

Published by Wildlife Education, Ltd.
12233 Thatcher Court, Poway, California 92064
contact us at: **1-800-477-5034**
e-mail us at: **animals@zoobooks.com**
visit us at: **www.zoobooks.com**

ISBN 1-932396-00-4

Seals and Sea Lions

Created and Written by
John Bonnett Wexo

Scientific Consultant
Hubbs-SeaWorld Research Institute

Art Credits

Pages Eight and Nine: Walter Stuart

Pages Ten and Eleven: Walter Stuart

Page Ten: Bottom Left, Graham Allen

Page Eleven: Top, Middle, and Bottom Right, Graham Allen

Pages Twelve and Thirteen: Walter Stuart

Page Twelve: Middle Left and Bottom Left: Graham Allen

Page Thirteen: Top Right and Bottom, Graham Allen

Pages Sixteen and Seventeen: Walter Stuart

Page Sixteen: Middle Left, Graham Allen

Page Seventeen: Top and Bottom Right, Graham Allen

Pages Twenty and Twenty-one: Walter Stuart

Page Twenty: Bottom Left, Graham Allen

Page Twenty-one: Top Right and Bottom Right, Graham Allen

Photographic Credits

Front Cover: Francois Gohier

Pages Six and Seven: G.L. Kooyman *(Animals Animals)*

Page Ten: Top, Cristopher Crowley *(Tom Stack & Associates)*; **Middle,** Kevin Schafer *(Tom Stack & Associates)*

Page Eleven: Kevin Schafer *(Tom Stack & Associates)*

Page Twelve: Top, C. Allan Morgan *(Peter Arnold, Inc.)*; **Middle,** Robert Evans *(Peter Arnold, Inc.)*

Page Thirteen: Middle Right, Bob Evans *(Peter Arnold, Inc.)*; **Middle Left,** Kevin Schafer *(Tom Stack & Associates)*

Pages Fourteen and Fifteen: John Matthews *(DRK Photo)*

Page Sixteen: Top, Jen and Des Bartlett *(Bruce Coleman, Inc.)*; **Middle Left,** Jen and Des Bartlett; **Bottom Left,** Jeff Foott *(Bruce Coleman, Inc.)*

Page Seventeen: E.R. Degginger *(Animals Animals)*

Pages Eighteen and Nineteen: Jim Zipp *(Photo Researchers)*

Page Twenty: Top, Leonard Lee Rue III *(Animals Animals)*; **Middle,** Tom Stack *(Tom Stack & Associates)*

Page Twenty-one: Top Right, Mark Newman *(Tom Stack & Associates)*; **Middle,** Med Beauregard *(PPS)*; **Bottom Left,** S.J. Krasemann *(DRK Photo)*

Pages Twenty-two and Twenty-three: Barry E. Parker *(Bruce Coleman, Inc.)*

On the Cover: A Harbor Seal

Contents

Seals, sea lions, and walruses live in two different worlds. They spend part of their lives on land and part of their lives in water. On land, they may look clumsy. In the water, they swim with a speed and grace that is wonderful to watch. In fact, many species swim so well that they seem to fly underwater.

To help them fly through the water, these animals have flippers instead of arms and legs. The flippers look like fins, or "wings," and this is why seals, sea lions, and walruses are all called *pinnipeds*, which means "wing-footed."

In general, pinnipeds have streamlined, cigar-shaped bodies that slip through the water easily. Strong muscles propel their bodies, and this helps to make these animals very good swimmers. Some pinnipeds swim long distances, and some dive deep to find food.

Pinnipeds are marine mammals. Like people and other land mammals, pinnipeds have lungs and must breathe air to stay alive. Like you and me, they are warm-blooded, with a body temperature that must be kept at a certain level all the time. Their babies are born alive like human babies, and the babies get milk from their mothers. Like many land mammals, pinnipeds have hair that covers their bodies.

Most pinnipeds live in cold places. For instance, many seals and walruses are found close to the North Pole. There are also seals in waters near the South Pole. In such places, seals often spend a long time swimming under huge blocks of ice looking for food.

Many people think of snow and ice when they think of seals and other pinnipeds. But there are seals and sea lions that live in warm places as well. There are sea lions in California, and seals in Hawaii and the Mediterranean Sea.

Adult male pinnipeds are called bulls. Adult females are called cows. Baby seals are called pups until they are about five months old, and then they are called yearlings. A young walrus is called a calf.

A WEDDELL SEAL SEARCHES FOR FOOD UNDER THE ICE.

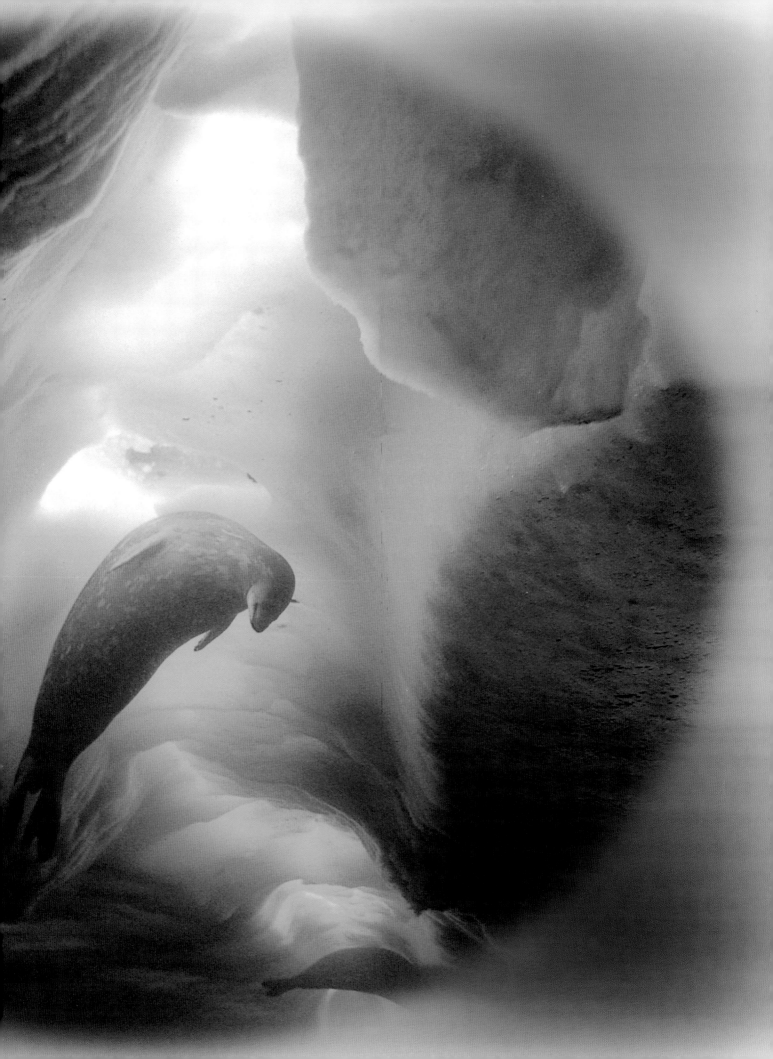

There is more variety among pinnipeds than you might expect. All of their bodies are the same general shape—but the shapes of their heads and the patterns of fur on their bodies can be very different. There is also a great variety of sizes. The biggest of all is the Elephant seal. Males of this species can be more than 16 feet long and weigh over 5,000 pounds.

WALRUS
Odobenus rosmarus

SOUTHERN SEA LION
Otaria byronia

NORTHERN FUR SEAL
Callorhinus ursinus

HARP SEAL AND PUP
Phoca groenlandica

RINGED SEAL
Phoca hispida

BEARDED SEAL
Erignathus barbatus

CRABEATER SEAL
Lobodon carcinophagus

WEDDELL SEAL
Leptonychotes weddelli

HOODED SEAL
Cystophora cristata

SOUTHERN ELEPHANT SEAL
Mirounga leonina

NORTHERN ELEPHANT SEAL
Mirounga angustirostris

LEOPARD SEAL
Hydrurga leptonyx

STELLER'S SEA LION
Eumetopius jubatus

RIBBON SEAL
Phoca fasciata

CALIFORNIA SEA LION
Zalophus californianus

MEDITERRANEAN MONK SEAL
Monachus monachus

The bodies of all pinnipeds do look much the same at first glance. All of them have long and rather streamlined bodies, shaped like fat submarines. They all have four flippers—one pair in front and one pair in the back. Almost all pinnipeds are covered with fur. They have long hairs on their faces that look like cat whiskers.

With so many things that are similar, you may think that it's going to be very hard for you to tell one kind of pinniped from another. But there are differences between them that are going to make it *easy* for you to tell one from another—and in only a few seconds!

The easiest pinniped to recognize is the walrus. For one thing, it is bigger than any other pinniped except the Elephant seal. And walruses are the only pinnipeds that have long tusks. You'll learn more about walruses later.

On these two pages, you can learn how to tell a seal from a sea lion or a fur seal.

When you see a pinniped, look at its head. Does it have ears? Sea lions and fur seals have tiny ear flaps, but true seals do not. For this reason, sea lions and fur seals are sometimes called "eared seals." Can you tell which of these two animals is a true seal and which is a sea lion?

TRUE SE

SEA LION

SEA LION

When sea lions and fur seals swim, they use their *front* flippers to push them through the water. Their rear flippers are used to help steer them, like the rudder on a boat.

TRUE SEAL

True seals use their *rear* flippers to push them when they swim. The front flippers are used for steering.

SEA LION

True seals can't use their rear flippers as feet. This makes them rather clumsy when they move around on land. Some species use their front flippers to pull them forward. Others hunch their bodies and move like inchworms. In spite of this, some types of seals may travel many miles on land. Some of them can even move fast. Crabeater seals are the fastest on land and can speed across snow as fast as 15 miles per hour.

TRUE SEAL

Sea lions and fur seals can use both pairs of their flippers to walk on land. They bring the rear flippers forward and use them as feet. This lets them move fairly well on land, but they are much more graceful in the water.

2

All pinnipeds can open and close their noses. When they stick their heads out of the water or come up on land, they can open their nostrils to breathe ①. But when they dive, the nostrils close to keep water out ②.

1

Because you live on land, the natural position for your nostrils is open. But pinnipeds spend a great deal of time underwater, so the natural position for their nostrils is closed. They have special muscles that can open the nostrils when they want to breathe. The moment they relax these muscles, the nostrils snap shut.

One reason why many pinnipeds look like chubby cigars is that they have a thick layer of fat under the skin. This fat helps to keep them warm when they swim in cold water or lie on snow and ice.

BLUBBER

WALRUS

The fat under the skin is called blubber. Walruses have more blubber than any other pinniped, and this is one reason why they are bigger. The fat on a large walrus can be six inches thick in places. The fat *alone* can weigh over 900 pounds!

11

True seals are the largest group of pinnipeds, with more different kinds than any other group. As you can see on the map at right, they also live in more places than any other pinnipeds.

No matter where they live, true seals stay alive by eating fish and other sea creatures. Like all pinnipeds, they are excellent hunters. They usually have no trouble catching all the smaller animals they can eat. In turn, seals and other pinnipeds are sometimes caught by animals that are larger than they are—such as Killer whales.

ATLANTIC OCEAN

PACIFIC OCEAN

Places where seals live are shown in yellow.

As a rule, male seals are larger than females. Can you find the male Elephant seal in this picture?

At mating time, the males of some species fight with each other. The males that win the most fights get the most females as mates.

It's easy to see how the Elephant seal got its name. The "trunks" on some large males can be more than 11 inches long. Sometimes, when the males get really angry, they may blow up their "trunks" like big balloons.

Killer whales have a clever way of capturing seals that are resting on ice floes. One whale pushes up the side of the ice (shown at left). The seal tumbles off—and lands in the open mouth of a second whale.

PACIFIC OCEAN

INDIAN
OCEAN

In general, seals and other pinnipeds live in certain places because they can find plenty of food there. Pinnipeds are near the top of the "food chain" in the ocean. This chain begins with very small animals and plants ①.

Near the top of the chain, fish that have been eating smaller animals are eaten in turn by pinnipeds ③.

3

Favorite foods of seals are squid and medium-sized fish.

The smallest animals and plants are eaten by slightly larger animals ②. These are eaten by still larger animals.

Life in the ocean can be dangerous for seals and other pinnipeds. In cold waters, Killer whales hunt them. In warmer waters, they are preyed upon by sharks.

To find food, a seal in cold waters may have to swim around under the ice for a long time. Some seals can hold their breath for *almost an hour*. Eventually, they have to find a hole in the ice so they can get some air.

Seals and most other pinnipeds have large eyes. Their eyes are adapted to low light. Light reflects through their eyes a second time. They see well deep in the ocean and out of the water.

Seals that use breathing holes usually have several of them. When ice forms over the holes, the seals dig it out with their teeth and claws. Sometimes they melt the new ice with their warm breath. Polar bears and Inuits—the people of the far north—often hunt seals by waiting at breathing holes. When the seals come to breathe, the hunters catch them.

13

Sea lions and fur seals are very closely related. They look so much alike and behave in such similar ways that scientists place them in the same family. There are some differences between them, though.

Sea lions usually have shorter snouts than fur seals. And the fur on sea lions is usually shorter and thinner. The fur on fur seals can be so long and thick that they are sometimes called "sea bears."

All adult male sea lions and fur seals are much larger than the females. Male sea lions often have manes of hair on their heads, as shown below.

PACIFIC OCEAN

Places where s lions and fur seals live are shown in yello

When they come out of the water, fur seals and sea lions usually choose rocky beaches as places to rest. Unlike seals and walruses, fur seals like this one don't like to lie down on snow and ice.

Sea lions got their name from the hairy manes that adult males have. These sometimes look much like the manes of African lions.

When a big male sea lion stalks down the beach on its flippers (below), it can look remarkably like an African lion.

Sea lion pups have to stay out of the way of the huge adult males. The males can have bad tempers, and they sometimes step on the young or injure them in other ways.

Like true seals, sea lions and fur seals may live in rather cold places. But most of them stay away from the coldest areas, near the North and South poles.

Sea lions and other pinnipeds may spend days in the water without going on land. They even sleep in the water. In shallow water, they sometimes sink to the bottom and sleep while holding their breath. They rise to the surface from time to time to get some air, then sink again. In deep water, they often float upright with just the tips of their noses above the water.

ATLANTIC OCEAN

PACIFIC OCEAN

INDIAN OCEAN

California sea lions and some other pinnipeds are famous for their ability to balance things on their noses. They learn these tricks fairly easily, indicating that they are intelligent animals. Some scientists think that pinnipeds may be as intelligent as cats or monkeys.

Skins of fur seals are sometimes made into coats. The fur is beautiful, but the skins look better on the seals, where they belong.

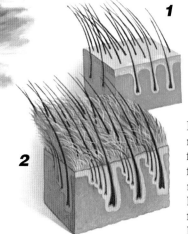

1

2

Fur seals have been killed by the millions to get their thick and soft fur. This fur is much thicker than the fur of other pinnipeds, because it has many more hairs. In addition to the long hairs that all pinnipeds have ①, fur seals also have many shorter hairs ②. The shorter hairs are called *underfur*.

17

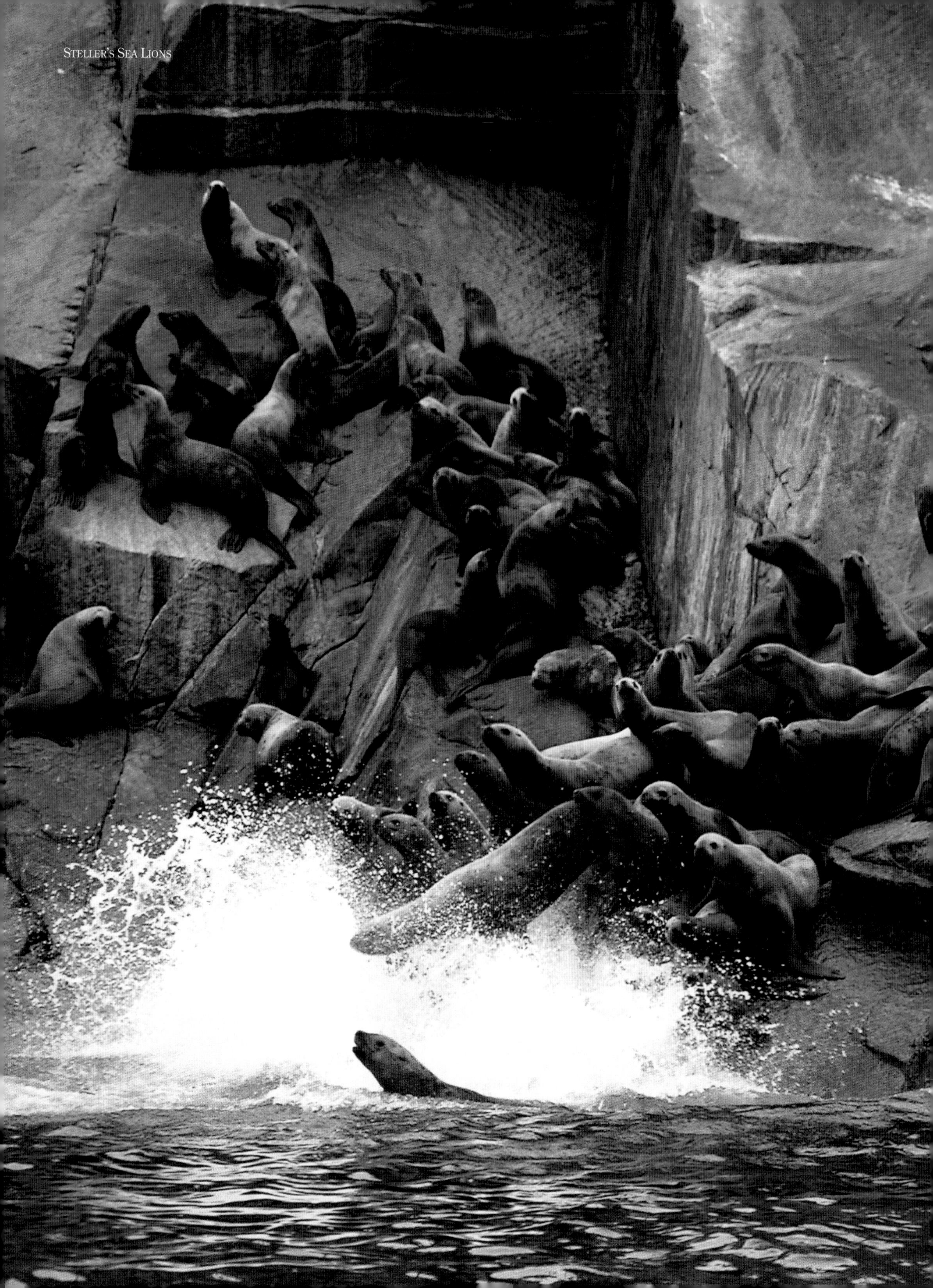

Walruses are really quite different from other pinnipeds in many ways. Unlike the others, walruses have long white tusks. They have short stiff whiskers, small piglike eyes, and the adult males have very little hair on their huge bodies.

Walruses are in a family all by themselves. Their closest living relatives are the fur seals, but they share some characteristics with both seals and sea lions. Like seals, they use their rear flippers to push them when they swim. But they also use their front flippers, like sea lions.

Male walruses can be very large. They are sometimes more than 12 feet long and the largest of them may weigh as much as 3,500 pounds. That's as much as *23 fully grown men*. Female walruses are smaller, but still rather large. They usually weigh about 1,500 pounds.

Almost all pinnipeds like to crowd together in large groups. When a group is in the water, it is called a herd. When it is on land, it is called a *rookery*.

All pinnipeds have little tails between their rear flippers. The walrus is the only one that has a flap of skin that connects the tail to the flippers.

The wonderful tusks of both male and female walruses are canine teeth in the upper jaw that grow very large. Throughout life, a walrus's tusks keep growing. A large walrus may have tusks three feet long. However, as walruses age, the lifelong wear and tear on their tusks results in shorter, blunter, and even broken tusks.

Walruses use their tusks to chop breathing holes in the ice, to defend themselves, and even to move onto an ice floe. By stabbing their tusks into the ice, they can pull their ponderous bodies forward. Part of the walrus's scientific name, *Odobenus*, means "tooth walk." Of the many uses for the tusks, the most important is as a visual symbol of a walrus's status in the herd. The largest walrus with the largest tusks is usually dominant.

All walruses live in the far north, where it can get very cold. Thick blubber keeps the walruses well-insulated against freezing temperatures. Walruses have been seen peacefully sleeping on the ice in a high wind and at a temperature of 31 degrees below zero.

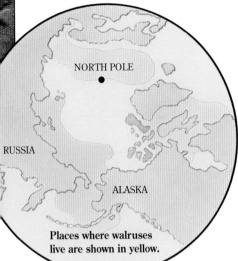

Places where walruses live are shown in yellow.

Walruses use "life preservers" when they are resting or sleeping at sea. Their thick blubber also helps them to float, because fat floats.

These life preservers are inflatable air pouches in their throats. The pouches help walruses to float in the water and also let them produce the special bell-like sounds of courtship.

Walrus whiskers are often used to find food. In the dark depths of the ocean, walruses use their whiskers to feel around in the mud for shrimps, snails, crabs, clams, and mussels. A walrus has about 300 thick, stubby whiskers.

The skin on the neck and shoulders of an adult male walrus is bumpy and about two inches thick. This offers protection against the stabbing tusks of other males.

The tusks of walruses are valuable. Like the tusks of elephants, they can be carved into art objects. For hundreds of years, people killed walruses for their ivory. This 12th-century chess piece is fashioned from walrus ivory.

Today, it is against the law in most countries to hunt walruses. The Inuits are still allowed to hunt them, because walrus meat and blubber are a traditional part of their food supply. By law, they cannot hunt with guns, but must use the traditional spears and methods of their culture. The peoples who share the top of the world with these marine mammals revere the walrus for its hardiness.

How does a walrus scratch its head? With its flipper, of course. Like all pinnipeds, the cumbersome-looking walrus has a very flexible backbone that helps it to make sharp turns when swimming—and when scratching.

The future of pinnipeds looks much brighter today than it once did. At one time, about 100 years ago, it seemed certain that almost all of the seals, sea lions, and walruses in the world would be destroyed by human hunters. Today, it appears that most species of pinnipeds are out of danger.

Hunting was not regulated during the 18th and 19th centuries, because little was known about the lives of pinnipeds. Whales and pinnipeds were hunted for the oil from their body fat. This oil was used in lamps before electric lights were invented. Millions of seals and other pinnipeds were used to provide oil for the lamps of the world. As a result, the numbers of many pinniped species fell rapidly Elephant seals came close to extinction. Some sea species did become extinct.

Many pinnipeds were also hunted for their fur. Fur seals of all kinds were almost wiped out. Walruses were killed for their bounteous oil and their beautiful ivory tusks. The north Atlantic population of walruses was so severely depleted that it never recovered. Luckily, the north Pacific population exists in healthy numbers.

Several things happened that helped to save the pinnipeds. First, species that were hunted to near extinction were left alone because their numbers were too low to justify the expense of hunting them. At the same time, electric lights were invented and the market for seal oil dwindled. Finally, governments around the world made laws to protect pinnipeds.

As a result of all these things, the numbers of most pinniped species have grown larger in recent years. With some species, such as Northern fur seals, there may be as many animals alive today as there were before all the hunting began.

Unlike the people of earlier centuries, we don't need oil from pinnipeds. And we have protective clothing that doesn't require the skins from wild animals. As we learn more about pinnipeds and all wild anmals, we realize that they have far more value for our future and the earth itself if they are alive.

Ironically, oil is still a danger to pinnipeds and all sea creatures. But this time it's not because they are hunted for their oil. The oil that endangers them today is from oil spills in the sea. The oil mats their fur and lowers their body temperatures. Oil is also ingested because it sticks to the foods they eat. This modern threat to pinnipeds and their environment is one we must work to prevent.

Index